PUBLISHER: LEVON MIRZOYAN VOSKE ART
EDITED AND FORMATTED BY THE PUBLISHER
SOURCE OF GRAPHICS: CANVA

Would You Rather

CHRISTMAS EDITION

2

WOULD YOU RATHER WORK IN
SANTA'S WORKSHOP

WORK IN A GIANT
TOY STORE?

WOULD YOU GO FOR A RIDE IN SANTA'S SLEIGH

TAKE A TRIP ON THE POLAR EXPRESS?

WOULD YOU RATHER DECORATE 100 CHRISTMAS TREES

DECORATE 100 CHRISTMAS COOKIES?

WOULD YOU RATHER HAVE A SNOWY CHRISTMAS

A HOT CHRISTMAS, WITH NO SNOW AT ALL?

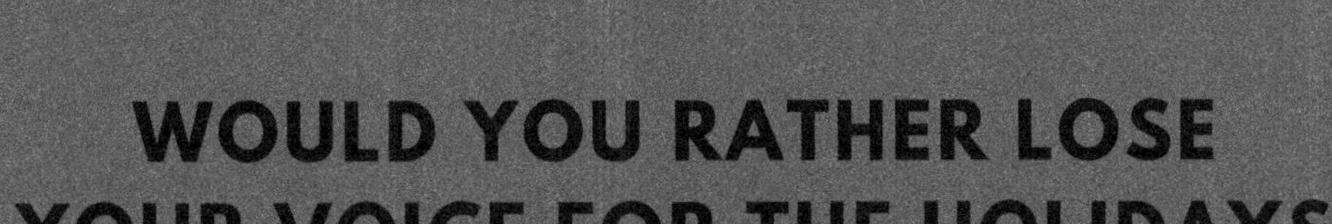

ONLY BE ABLE TO SPEAK IN CHRISTMAS CAROLS?

WOULD YOU RATHER SANTA'S RED SUIT TO SCHOOL

WEAR A GREEN ELF SUIT TO SCHOOL?

WOULD YOU RATHER EAT CHRISTMAS DINNER AT HOME

HELP SERVE CHRISTMAS DINNER TO THOSE WHO ARE LESS FORTUNATE?

WOULD YOU RATHER ONLY BE ALLOWED TO LISTEN TO CHRISTMAS CAROLS FOR A YEAR

HAVE TO MAKE TOYS FOR A YEAR?

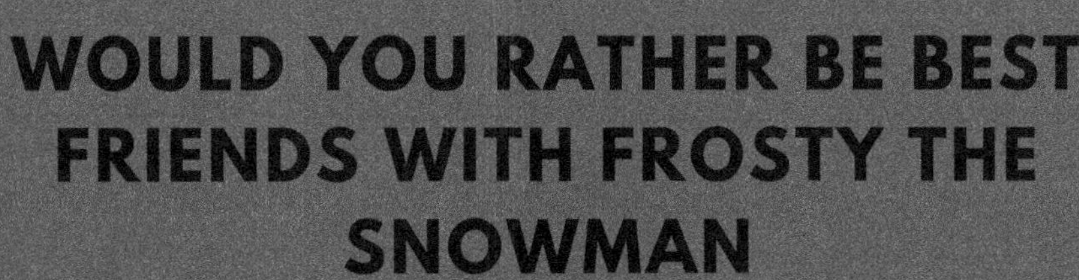

WOULD YOU RATHER BE BEST FRIENDS WITH FROSTY THE SNOWMAN

RUDOLPH THE RED NOSED REINDEER?

WOULD YOU RATHER BE ONE OF SANTA'S REINDEER

BE ONE OF SANTA'S ELVES?

WOULD YOU RATHER RECEIVE
ONE BIG PRESENT

RECEIVE 10 SMALL PRESENTS?

WOULD YOU RATHER OPEN YOUR PRESENTS ON CHRISTMAS EVE

ON CHRISTMAS MORNING?

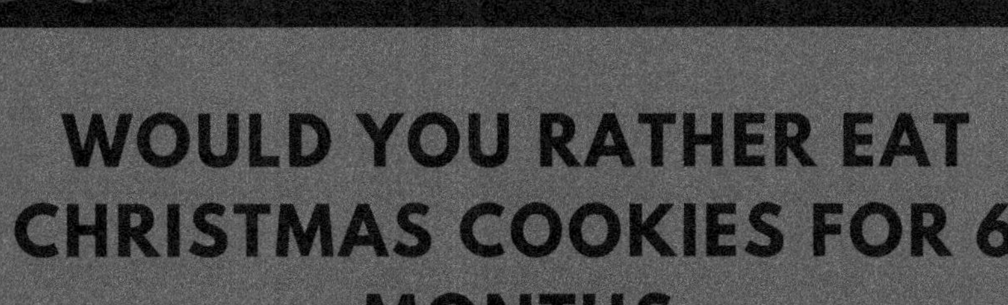

WOULD YOU RATHER EAT CHRISTMAS COOKIES FOR 6 MONTHS

Or

EAT CANDY CANES FOR 6 MONTHS?

WOULD YOU RATHER HAVE A RED NOSE THAT LIGHTS UP

HAVE POINTY ELF EARS?

WOULD YOU RATHER DRINK ONLY EGGNOG ALL DECEMBER

EAT CANDY CANES ALL DECEMBER?

WOULD YOU RATHER BE A MOUSE AND RECEIVE A BIG PIECE OF CHEESE FOR CHRISTMAS

BE A CAT AND RECEIVE A BIG FISH FOR CHRISTMAS?

WOULD YOU RATHER
CHRISTMAS CAROLING

Or

GO SLEDDING?

WOULD YOU RATHER HAVE TURKEY FOR CHRISTMAS DINNER

HAVE A HAM FOR CHRISTMAS DINNER?

WOULD YOU RATHER WEAR SANTA'S BIG BOOTS TO GYM CLASS

WEAR POINTY ELF SHOES TO GYM CLASS?

WOULD YOU RATHER BE RUDOLPH THE RED NOSED REINDEER

PRANCER, OR DANCER, OR BLITZEN?

WOULD YOU RATHER SPEND A DAY WITH MRS. CLAUS

SANTA CLAUS?

WOULD YOU RATHER EAT CHRISTMAS COOKIES FOR 6 MONTHS

EAT CANDY CANES FOR 6 MONTHS?

WOULD YOU RATHER BE MRS. CLAUS

BE THE HEAD ELF IN SANTA'S WORKSHOP?

WOULD YOU RATHER LIVE AT THE NORTH POLE

LIVE AT THE SOUTH POLE?

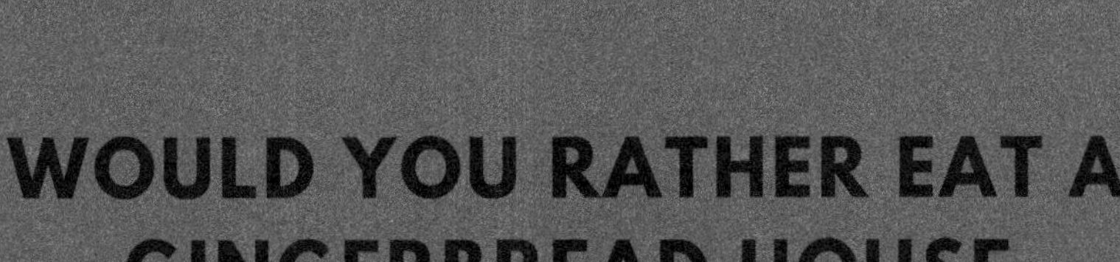

WOULD YOU RATHER EAT A GINGERBREAD HOUSE

LIVE IN A GINGERBREAD HOUSE?

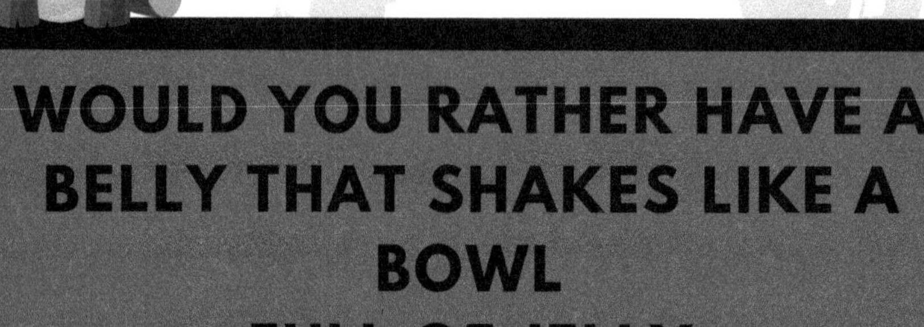

WOULD YOU RATHER HAVE A BELLY THAT SHAKES LIKE A BOWL FULL OF JELLY

EAT A BOWL FULL OF JELLY?

WOULD YOU RATHER BE A MELTING SNOWMAN

A MUNCHED ON GINGERBREAD PERSON?

WOULD YOU RATHER MAKE TOYS ALL YEAR LONG

PLAY WITH TOYS ALL YEAR LONG?

WOULD YOU RATHER EAT CHRISTMAS COOKIES WITH SANTA

BAKE CHRISTMAS COOKIES WITH SANTA?

WOULD YOU RATHER SPEND 2 DAYS COOKING A GIANT CHRISTMAS MEAL

2 DAYS CLEANING UP AFTER THE CHRISTMAS MEAL?

WOULD YOU RATHER NEVER EAT CANDY AGAIN

NEVER PLAY IN THE SNOW AGAIN?

WOULD YOU RATHER BE ARRESTED FOR IMPERSONATING SANTA CLAUS

FOR STEALING PRESENTS?

WOULD YOU RATHER NEVER HAVE HOT CHOCOLATE AGAIN

NEVER WATCH A CHRISTMAS MOVIE EVER AGAIN?

WOULD YOU RATHER GIVE ONE PERSON A $1,000

GIVE 1,000 PEOPLE A $1 GIFT?

WOULD YOU RATHER HAVE ELF EARS

SANTA'S WHITE BEARD FOREVER?

WOULD YOU RATHER SIT IN A TUB OF HOT CHOCOLATE FOR 6 HOURS

TRY TO STUFF 100 MARSHMALLOWS IN YOUR MOUTH?

WOULD YOU RATHER STAR IN THE WORLD'S WORST CHRISTMAS MOVIE

DRESS AS MRS. CLAUS FOR A YEAR?

WOULD YOU RATHER ONLY BE ABLE TO SPEAK IN CHRISTMAS SONG LYRICS

Or

ONLY BE ABLE TO SPEAK IN CHRISTMAS MOVIE QUOTES?

WOULD YOU RATHER HAVE HOLIDAY DECORATIONS UP ALL YEAR

NEVER BE ABLE TO PUT THEM UP AGAIN?

WOULD YOU RATHER SHOP FOR 3,000 GIFTS

WRAP 3,000 GIFTS.

WOULD YOU RATHER HAVE SANTA CLAUS SNEEZE IN YOUR FACE

HAVE A REINDEER POOP ON YOUR SHOES?

WOULD YOU RATHER CELEBRATE CHRISTMAS EVERY MONTH

ONCE EVERY 10 YEARS?

WOULD YOU RATHER SING CHRISTMAS SONGS SOLO TO AN AUDIENCE OF 3 MILLION PEOPLE

WET YOUR PANTS WHILE SITTING ON SANTA'S LAP?

WOULD YOU RATHER HAVE CANDY CANES FOR FINGERS

GUMDROPS FOR EYES?

WOULD YOU RATHER GIVE YOUR CRUSH A THREE-YEAR-OLD FRUIT CAKE

A PAIR OF USED CHRISTMAS SOCKS?

WOULD YOU RATHER READ A 2,000-PAGE BOOK ABOUT CHRISTMAS

WRITE A 2,000-PAGE BOOK ABOUT CHRISTMAS?

WOULD YOU RATHER KISS A POLAR BEAR

KISS A COMPLETE STRANGER UNDER THE MISTLETOE?

WOULD YOU RATHER GET ACCIDENTALLY LOCKED IN THE MALL

STUCK AT THE AIRPORT ON CHRISTMAS?

WOULD YOU RATHER HAVE A BIG BELLY LIKE SANTA CLAUS

HAVE A BIG GLOWING RED NOSE LIKE RUDOLPH?

WOULD YOU RATHER HAVE TO RING THE SALVATION ARMY BELL FOR 48 HOURS STRAIGHT

RECEIVE 48 AWFUL GIFTS THAT YOU CAN'T RETURN?

WOULD YOU RATHER FALL INTO A HOLLY BUSH

SIT ON A SHARPENED CANDY CANE?

WOULD YOU RATHER HAVE SKIS FOR FEET

TINSEL FOR HAIR?

WOULD YOU RATHER DECORATE YOUR HOME WITH CHRISTMAS GARLAND MADE FROM SOMEONE ELSE'S DIRTY UNDERWEAR

DECORATE YOUR TREE WITH WET CAT FOOD?

WOULD YOU RATHER ACCIDENTALLY BREAK THE WORLD'S MOST EXPENSIVE CHRISTMAS TREE ORNAMENT

STEAL SANTA'S SLEIGH?

WOULD YOU RATHER BE TURNED INTO A REAL DONKEY FOR A NATIVITY PLAY

SING JINGLE BELLS VERY LOUDLY FOR AN HOUR IN A LIBRARY?

WOULD YOU RATHER KNIT A SWEATER MADE OF SANTA'S BEARD HAIR

WEAR A SWEATER MADE OF SANTA'S BEARD HAIR?

WOULD YOU RATHER LOSE ALL OF YOUR LUGGAGE

LOSE ALL THE GIFTS YOU BOUGHT AT THE AIRPORT?

WOULD YOU RATHER HAVE A CARROT FOR A NOSE

REINDEER HOOF HANDS?

WOULD YOU RATHER LAUGH 'HO HO HO!' AS YOUR USUAL LAUGH

HAVE A HIGH SQUEAKY VOICE LIKE AN ELF?

WOULD YOU RATHER BE THE ONLY PERSON TO NOT RECEIVE A GIFT

BE THE ONLY PERSON THAT GAVE GIFTS?

WOULD YOU RATHER GET STUCK IN A CHIMNEY FOR FOUR HOURS

WEAR A DIFFERENT UGLY CHRISTMAS SWEATER EVERY DAY FOR FOUR MONTHS?

WOULD YOU RATHER HAVE TO WRITE SANTA'S 'NAUGHTY OR NICE' LIST

HAVE TO CHECK THE LIST TWICE FOR HIM?

WOULD YOU RATHER DECORATE AN 80-FT TALL GINGERBREAD MAN

BAKE A 1-TON FRUITCAKE?

WOULD YOU RATHER RECEIVE AN OFFENSIVE CHRISTMAS CARD FROM YOUR GRANDMOTHER

GIVE AN OFFENSIVE CHRISTMAS CARD TO YOUR GRANDMOTHER?

WOULD YOU RATHER HAVE A HALLOWEEN PARTY?

HAVE A CHRISTMAS PARTY?

WOULD YOU RATHER MAKE TOYS IN THE WORKSHOP?

DELIVER TOYS ALL OVER THE WORLD?

WOULD YOU RATHER TRAIN THE REINDEER?

BE THE HEAD ELF?

WOULD YOU RATHER MEET THE GRINCH?

SHOVEL SNOW FOR 5 HOURS?

www.ingramcontent.com/pod-product-compliance
Lightning Source LLC
Chambersburg PA
CBHW082204231225
37245CB00020B/207

* 9 7 9 8 5 7 0 1 8 7 1 6 0 *